GO FACTS TRANSPORT
Planes

A & C BLACK • LONDON

Planes

© Blake Publishing 2003
Additional material © A & C Black Publishers Ltd 2005

First published 2003 in Australia by Blake Education Pty Ltd

This edition published 2005 in the United Kingdom by
A & C Black Publishers Ltd, 37 Soho Square, London W1D 3QZ
www.acblack.com

ISBN-10: 0-7136-7273-0
ISBN-13: 978-0-7136-7273-2

A CIP record for this book is available from the British Library.

Written by Ian Rohr
Design and layout by The Modern Art Production Group
Photos by Photodisc, Corel, Corbis, Photo Alto, Digital Stock, Brand X,
Comstock and Eyewire.
Cover photo by BAA Aviation Photo Library.

UK series consultant: Julie Garnett

Printed in China by WKT Company Ltd.

A & C Black uses paper produced with elemental chlorine-free pulp,
harvested from managed sustainable forests.

Contents

What Is a Plane?

A plane is a machine that flies. All planes have engines, wheels and wings.

Planes are made in many sizes. They range from one-person planes to big jet planes that carry hundreds of people. Some of the biggest planes carry tonnes of cargo.

Plane engine

Planes are the fastest kind of transport. People used to take months to travel thousands of miles. Now, it can be done in one day.

Only two people can fly in this plane.

Planes can take off and land by day or night.

The pilot and the co-pilot sit in the cockpit.

People and Flying

People have been flying for more than 200 years.

Long ago, people studied birds and insects to see how they fly. Then they made kites, hot-air balloons, gliders and blimps.

Orville and Wilbur Wright made and flew the first **biplane** in 1903. Biplanes have two sets of wings to help lift the plane off the ground.

The first planes had **propellers**. Now most planes have **jet engines**.

Glider

Biplanes can be used to spray crops.

GO FACT!

FIRST!

The first kites were made over 2300 years ago in China.

Today, people still design and make planes.

Types of Planes

Different planes carry people or cargo on short trips or to faraway places.

The smallest planes are propeller planes. The largest and most powerful planes are jet planes. They have up to four engines and carry more that 500 people. Jumbo jets can fly for about 14 hours without stopping.

Seaplanes can land on water. For many years the largest passenger planes were seaplanes.

Propeller plane

Jumbo jets have 18 wheels and more than 6 million parts.

Seaplanes are sometimes used in places where there are no airports.

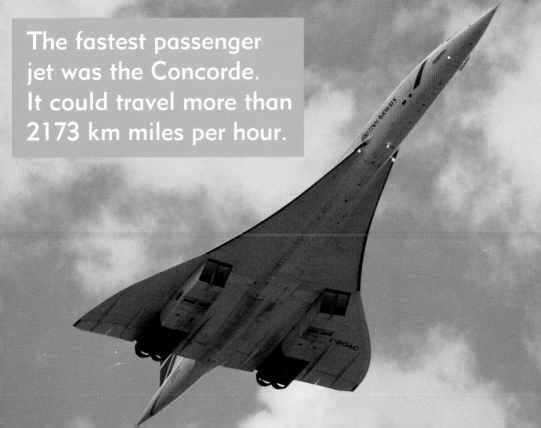

The fastest passenger jet was the Concorde. It could travel more than 2173 km miles per hour.

Moving People

Planes take people all around the world.

Most planes take off and land at airports. Hundreds of passenger planes arrive and depart every day from large airports.

Jumbo jets are the biggest kind of passenger plane. People travel on them for work, or to go on holiday. Some jumbo jet flights cover long distances and take many hours. Passengers can eat, sleep and watch films **onboard**.

Luggage tags

Very large 747 jet planes are called jumbos.

Large airports have many gates for planes.

GO FACT!

FIRST!
The first passenger-carrying airline began in Florida in 1914.

Passengers are given safety instructions before take off.

Moving Goods

Planes move goods as well as people. Goods transported on planes are called cargo.

Cargo planes are very big. Some cargo planes carry goods that need to arrive quickly, such as mail, food and medicine. Others carry unusual cargo such as flowers, horses and live lobsters.

When floods, tornadoes or earthquakes happen, planes are used to bring in emergency supplies. These supplies can often save people's lives.

Service vehicles

The ground crews take cargo and luggage to the planes.

BIGGEST!
The Antonov AN–225 can hold 80 cars, and its wingspan is almost as long as a football field.

Cargo is loaded onto a plane through an opening called a hatch.

13

Military Planes

The air force uses fighter planes and helicopters in battles, and transport planes to move troops and supplies.

Sea Knight helicopters

Fighter planes are built to be very fast. They turn and dive easily while flying at high speeds.

Helicopters are powered by a **rotor**. A rotor is like a big propeller that spins on top of the helicopter. Helicopters can **hover** in the air. They can also take off and land without a runway.

14

Soldiers practise exercises beneath a military helicopter.

Stealth bombers are able to hide from enemy radar.

Military planes often perform at air shows.

Glossary

biplane	a plane with two sets of wings
hover	stay in one spot in midair
jet engine	an engine that uses a stream of hot gases to push the plane forward
onboard	within a vehicle
propeller	blades that turn like a fan to move a vehicle
rotor	the blades on a helicopter
seaplane	a plane that can take off and land on water

Index